KISS HER, YOU BLOCKHEAD!

BONK!

KISS HER, YOU BLOCKHEAD!

by Charles M. Schulz

An Owl Book
Henry Holt and Company / New York

Henry Holt and Company, Inc.
Publishers since 1866
115 West 18th Street
New York, New York 10011

Henry Holt® is a registered trademark
of Henry Holt and Company, Inc.

Library of Congress Catalog Card Number: 89-81383

ISBN 0-8050-1343-1 (An Owl Book: pbk.)

Henry Holt books are available for special promotions
and premiums. For details contact: Director, Special Markets.

New Owl Book Edition—1990

Printed in the United States of America
All first editions are printed on acid-free paper.∞

3   5   7   9   10   8   6   4

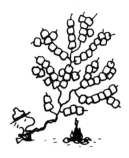

I ALWAYS WONDERED WHAT HAPPENED TO OLD WORN-OUT HIRED HANDS

HERE, PARTNER, LET'S SEE YOU HIT A FEW SERVES...

YOUR HANDS LOOK KIND OF SMALL, AND YOU DON'T HAVE ANY POCKETS...

HOW'RE YOU GONNA HOLD TWO BALLS WHEN YOU SERVE?

LOOK WHO WE PLAY IN THE FIRST ROUND... "CRYBABY" BOOBIE AND "BAD CALL" BENNY!

BOOBIE COMPLAINS ABOUT EVERYTHING, AND BENNY CALLS EVERYTHING "OUT"!

I REMEMBER THE LAST TIME I PLAYED AGAINST HIM...

AS SOON AS I OPENED THE CAN OF BALLS, HE CALLED THEM "OUT"!

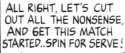

Beauty Tips

Always remember that beauty is only skin deep.

fur deep.

Beauty Tips

Always remember that beauty is only fur deep.

feather deep.

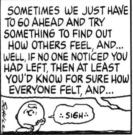

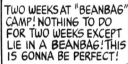

HERE'S THE WORLD FAMOUS ATTORNEY ON HIS WAY TO THE TRIAL...

IF YOU'RE GOING TO COURT, YOU SHOULD REMEMBER THIS...

"THAT WHICH OUGHT TO HAVE BEEN DONE IS TO BE REGARDED AS DONE, IN FAVOR OF HIM IN WHOM, AND AGAINST HIM FROM WHOM, PERFORMANCE IS DUE!"

THAT WON'T EVEN FIT IN MY BRIEFCASE!

YES, MA'AM..HE'S AN ATTORNEY

HE WANTS TO ORDER AN 8½-INCH X 11¾-INCH CANARY YELLOW, FIFTY-PAGE LEGAL PAD...

ANYTHING ELSE?

HE WANTS TO KNOW IF YOU HAVE ANYONE YOU WANT SUED...

THIS PROGRAM WILL BE REPEATED AT THIS SAME TIME TOMORROW...

...IN CASE YOU FELL ASLEEP

BAM! BAM! BAM!

IS IT SUPPERTIME ALREADY?

I'M SORRY...YOU MAY NOT BELIEVE THIS, BUT I WAS READING THE BOOK OF PSALMS, AND FORGOT WHAT TIME IT WAS...

WHAT ARE YOU DOING?

NOW WHAT?

PSALM FIFTY... VERSE TWELVE..."IF I WERE HUNGRY, I WOULD NOT TELL THEE"

GIVE ME TWO WEEKS, AND I'LL FIND A VERSE TO ANSWER YOU!

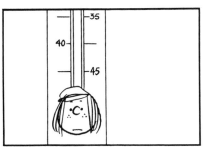

MANAGER'S OFFICE
THE BUCK STARTS
HERE.....

OKAY, TEAM, LET'S PAY ATTENTION!

LAST YEAR WE HAD TOO MANY PLAYERS GETTING HIT ON THE HEAD WITH FLY BALLS...

LET'S SEE IF WE CAN'T CHANGE THAT THIS YEAR

WHAP!

BONK! BONK! BONK!

MAYBE YOU SHOULDN'T ALL BE STANDING IN A ROW LIKE THAT...

SPREAD OUT A LITTLE, AND WE'LL TRY IT AGAIN...

WHAP!

BONK!

GOOD! THAT WAS A LOT BETTER!

YOU'RE LOOKING FOR YOUR PIANO, RIGHT?

GUESS WHAT.. I WASHED IT!

YOU **WHAT**?

I'LL BET THAT PIANO HASN'T BEEN CLEANED IN TWO YEARS... I PUT IT IN THE WASHER..

YOU CAN'T PUT A PIANO IN THE WASHER!

DON'T GET SO EXCITED! IT CAME OUT FINE...

FROM A **WASHER**?!!

I WILL ADMIT ONE THING, HOWEVER...

I DON'T THINK I SHOULD HAVE PUT IT IN THE DRYER..

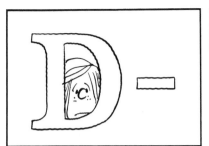

I HATE IT WHEN THEY ALL TALK AT ONCE!

"JOHNNY MILLER ALL THE WAY"

"...FOUR TO THREE IN TEN INNINGS"

"AND THAT'S SPORTS FOR TONIGHT"

THAT'S SPORTS ?!! WHAT DO YOU MEAN, THAT'S SPORTS ?!!

ALL YOU TOLD US ABOUT WERE MEN! WHAT ABOUT WOMEN IN SPORTS ?!!!

YOU DIDN'T SAY ANYTHING ABOUT JOANNE CARNER, OR SALLY LITTLE, OR HOLLIS STACY, OR BILLIE JEAN KING, OR ROSIE CASALS OR SHARON WALSH! AND WHAT ABOUT DONNA ADAMEK, BETH HEIDEN OR MARY DECKER ?

DID YOU TELL US WHAT CONNI PLACE HAS BEEN DOING? AND HOW ABOUT ALISON ROWE, AND TRACY CAULKINS, AND KAREN ROGERS, AND EVELYN ASHFORD, AND ANN MEYERS, AND JUDY SLADKY AND SARAH DOCTER ?!

DID YOU SAY ANYTHING ABOUT JENNIFER HARDING OR SHIRLEY MULDOWNEY ? WHAT DO YOU MEAN, "THAT'S SPORTS" ?!!

WHAT DO YOU WANT TO WATCH NEXT, SIR? THERE'RE SOME OLD MOVIES ON THE OTHER CHANNELS..

"THE MEN," "A MAN FOR ALL SEASONS" AND "ALL THE KING'S MEN"

I CAN'T STAND IT...

DO YOU LIKE BIRD STORIES? HERE'S A BIRD STORY...

THERE WAS THIS LITTLE BIRD, SEE, AND HE HAD BEEN VERY BAD..HIS MOTHER HAD YELLED AT HIM, AND HE FELT AWFUL...

HE WAS DEPRESSED AND ANGRY, AND HE DIDN'T KNOW WHAT TO DO...

"ALL RIGHT!" HE SHOUTED.."IF NO ONE AROUND HERE LIKES ME, I'LL JUST GO OUT IN THE BACKYARD AND EAT WORMS!"

"IF YOU DO THAT," SAID HIS MOTHER, "YOU'LL SPOIL YOUR DINNER!"

HEE HEE HEE HEE

SCHULZ

:SIGH:

HI! I THOUGHT MAYBE IT WAS YOU...

I'VE BEEN WATCHING YOU FROM WAY OFF... YOU'RE LOOKING GREAT...

THAT'S NICE TO KNOW

THE SECRET OF LIFE IS TO LOOK GOOD AT A DISTANCE

RING!

GOOD MORNING, MY NAME IS LINUS VAN PELT..I'M HERE TO TELL YOU ABOUT THE "GREAT PUMPKIN"

SLAM!

GOOD MORNING.. MY NAME IS LINUS VAN PELT...TODAY IS HALLOWEEN, AND I'M HERE TO TELL YOU ABOUT THE "GREAT PUMPKIN"

SLAM!

GOOD MORNING, MY NAME IS LINUS VAN PELT, AND I'M HERE TO TELL YOU ABOUT THE "GREAT PUMPKIN"

SLAM!

GOOD MORNING... MY NAME IS..

SLAM!

SLAM!!

SLAM!

Dear Great Pumpkin,
I visited fifty homes today to tell them about you. They all slammed their doors in my face. But at least I tried.
Sincerely,
Linus Van Pelt

SLAM!

YES, MA'AM, THIS IS A LOOSE-LEAF BINDER THAT I HAVE ON MY HEAD

WELL, YOU SEE, IT WAS RAINING ON MY WAY TO SCHOOL THIS MORNING..

NO, MA'AM, I REALLY CAN'T TAKE IT OFF BECAUSE..

YIPE!

BECAUSE MY HAIR IS CAUGHT IN THE BINDER..

SHE GOT IT OFF! MARCIE GOT IT OFF! WHEW! WHAT A RELIEF!

MY HOMEWORK? IT'S RIGHT HERE IN MY BINDER THAT I PUT OVER MY HEAD WHEN MY HAIR GOT ALL WET FROM WALKING TO SCHOOL IN THE RAIN

DON'T SIGH LIKE THAT, MA'AM.. IT BREAKS MY HEART...

I HEARD SOMEONE ON TV SAY THAT THE WORLD IS GETTING WORSE EVERY DAY

THAT'S RIDICULOUS!

HOW COULD THE WORLD BE GETTING WORSE WITH ME IN IT? EVER SINCE I WAS BORN THE WORLD HAS SHOWN A DISTINCT IMPROVEMENT!

I MAKE THE WORLD BETTER! I'M A POSITIVE FORCE!

SMILE!

SEE? WITH ME AROUND, EVERYONE IS A LOT HAPPIER!

PUT AWAY THAT HISTORY BOOK, MARCIE...ART IS NEXT!

I LOVE ART CLASS!

HOW'S THIS, MA'AM? TWENTY-FOUR COWS STANDING IN A PASTURE.. EACH ONE RENDERED IN EXQUISITE DETAIL!

MAYBE I'LL ADD SOME SHEEP, AND RABBITS AND SQUIRRELS...

AH! A GORGEOUS PASTORAL SETTING!

NOW, I'LL COLOR THE SKY BLUE, THE GRASS GREEN AND PUT IN SOME YELLOW FLOWERS..

WOW! WHAT A PICTURE! WHAT AN ARTISTIC TRIUMPH!

MARCIE! YOU HAVEN'T DRAWN A THING!

SOME OF US ARE JUST PATRONS OF THE ARTS, SIR

THE COURT WILL NOT AID THOSE WHO HAVE COMMITTED ILLEGAL ACTS IN A MATTER...

..AND THEN ASK THE COURT'S HELP TO RECOVER FOR ANY INJURY THEY MAY HAVE SUFFERED AS A RESULT THEREOF!

RATS!

ENTER OUR CONTEST NOW!

THE WINNER WILL RECEIVE FIFTY THOUSAND DOLLARS

THAT WINNER COULD BE YOU!!

BUT I DOUBT IT

THEY TOOK AWAY YOUR BASEBALL FIELD, CHARLES, AND YOU'RE NOT DOING ANYTHING ABOUT IT?

IS THIS HOW YOU'RE FIGHTING BACK... BY BOUNCING THAT STUPID GOLF BALL AGAINST THOSE STUPID STEPS?

WHAT DO YOU EXPECT ME TO DO?!

DON'T SCREAM, CHARLES.. IT'S EMBARRASSING...

I FIND IT DIFFICULT TO BELIEVE THAT THEY'VE TAKEN AWAY YOUR BALL FIELD, CHARLES, AND YOU'RE NOT FIGHTING BACK...

I FIND IT DIFFICULT TO BELIEVE THAT SOMEONE I AM VERY FOND OF COULD BE ACTING THIS WAY...

YOU'RE FOND OF **ME**?!

KISS HER, YOU BLOCKHEAD!

SCHULZ

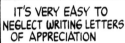
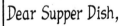